M000032255

AVOCUDDLE

An Hachette UK Company
www.hachette.co.uk

First published in Great Britain in 2019 by Pyramid,
an imprint of Octopus Publishing Group Ltd
Carmelite House, 50 Victoria Embankment,
London EC4Y 0DZ
www.octopusbooks.co.uk

ISBN 978-0-7537-3361-5

A CIP catalogue record for this book is available from
the British Library

Printed and bound in China

10 9 8 7 6 5 4 3 2 1

Publisher: Lucy Pessell
Designer: Lisa Layton
Editor: Sarah Vaughan
Assistant Production Manager: Lucy Carter

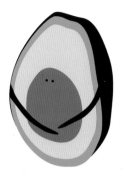

AVOCUDDLE

comfort words for when
you're feeling downbeet

To: ....

From: ....

YOU BRING

CHIA TO MY LIFE

YOU ARE
SOMEONE'S
RAISIN TO SMILE

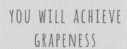

YOU WILL ACHIEVE
GRAPENESS

I WILL ALWAYS
BAYLEAF IN YOU

IT'S THYME TO TURNIP THE BEETS

AND GIVE YOURSELF A HIGH CHIVE

OH MY GOURD
YOU'RE AWESOME

YOU'RE NOT THE ONLY
PERSON IN THE UNIVERSE,
BUT YOU'RE THE ONION
THAT MATTERS

NEVER FIGET THAT I LOVE YOU

I YAM ALWAYS HERE FOR YOU

YOU WILL ALWAYS
BE MY FIRST CHOYS

I CHERRYSH YOU

DO THINGS TO
SALSIFY YOUR OWN SOUL

JUSTIN GAFFREY

THYME IS PRECIOUS,
SO ARE YOU

HOLY SHIITAKE
YOU ARE AWESOME

PEAS ROMAINE CALM AND CARROT ON

YOU CAN AND YOU SHOULD
ENDIVE YOU'RE BRAVE
ENOUGH TO START, YOU WILL

STEPHEN KING

YOU HAVE
ALL OF MY ENCOURAGEMINT

IF YOU ARE
GOING TO
RICE, YOU
MIGHT AS
WELL SHINE

LETTUCE NEVER BE PARTED

YOU ARE THE
YIN TO MY YAM

LIFE IS A
JOURNEY AND
ONLY YOU HOLD THE KIWI

IN ORDER TO SUCCEED,
WE MUST FIRST BAYLEAF THAT WE CAN

YOU'RE AWESOME TO THE CORE

THERE IS NO
"ME"
WITHOUT
"YOU".
YOU ARE MY
MISSING PEAS

THERE'S SO MUSHROOM
IN MY HEART FOR YOU

THERE ARE SO MANY
RAISINS TO BE HAPPY

YOUR SMILE IS
LIKE THE SUNRICE

PEAS BE WITH YOU

HAVE A HUG.
JUST COS

Sprout wings and fly

YOU CORN
COUNT ON ME

YOU FIGGIN ROCK

"HEY MR TANGERINE MAN, PLAY A STRAWBERRY..."

BOB DYLAN

#wejammin

YOU'RE SO SWEDE

I MINT WHAT I SAID,
YOU ARE AWESOME

YOU HAVE NO IDEA
HOW HARD IT IS
TO FORCE MYSELF
TO STOP THINKING
ABOUT YUZU
SOMETIMES

You're a little gem

BEETROOT TO YOURSELF

DON'T DISPEAR,
I AM THERE

ENDIVE I ASKED
YOU TO NAME ALL
THE THINGS THAT
YOU LOVE, HOW
LONG WOULD IT
TAKE FOR YOU TO
NAME YOURSELF?

Olive you with all my heart

I'll be there to cashew if you fall

YOU ARE BEETROOTIFUL...

MY QUEEN BEET

YOU'RE JUST PEARFECT

ALOE
SUNSHINE!

YOU ARE AMAIZEING

BEING FRIENDS
WITH YUZU MAKES
EVERY MORNING WORTH
GETTING UP FOR

IT'S ABOUT
LOVING WHAT YOU HAVE
AND BEING GRAPEFUL FOR IT

DON'T WORRY BE HAPPEA

YOU MAKE MISO

FIGGIN HAPPY

WORRYING DOES
NOT TAKE AWAY
TOMORROW'S
TROUBLES, IT
TAKES AWAY
TODAY'S PEAS

IF YOU
BAYLEAF IN
YOURSELF,
ANYTHING IS
POSSIBLE

DON'T BERRY YOUR FEELINGS

PEAS KNOW
HOW GRAPE YOU ARE

DO WHATEVER
FLOATS YOUR OAT

LETTUCE
ALWAYS
ROMAINE
TOGETHER

IT IS SAD TO GROW OLD
BUT NICE TO RIPEN

BRIGITTE BARDOT

YOU'RE THE ZEST

DON'T FIGET

TO BREATHE

SOY I'VE BEAN
THINKING OF YOU

**TOMARROW
IS A NEW DAY**

I'D GUAVA BE NEXT TO YOU

I WOULDN'T CHIANGE A
THING ABOUT YOU

MY HEART BEETS FOR YOU

LOVE LIKE THERE'S NO
TOMORROW ENDIVE
TOMORROW NEVER
COMES, LOVE AGAIN

"I BAYLEAF IN
MIRACLES,
SINCE YOU CAME
ALONG..."

HOT CHOCOLATE

FIND JOY IN THE LENTIL THINGS

CELERYBRATE THE
GOOD THYMES

AND NEVER CELERY
YOURSELF SHORT

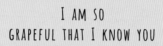

I AM SO
GRAPEFUL THAT I KNOW YOU

BREATHE, SMILE, AND GO CARPE THE SHIITAKE OUT OF THIS DIEM

MAKE EACH DAY
YOUR MASTERPEAS

THE SUN WILL
COME OUT TOMARROW

WORLD PEACE

BEGINS WITH INNER PEAS

YOU MUST ROMAINE
CALM ON YOUR
JOURNEY TO GRAPENESS

LES BROWN

IGNORE THE
HUSTLE AND BRUSSEL

ALOE YOU VERA MUCH

YOU ARE
24 CARROT GOLD

IT DOESN'T
MATTER HOW
SLOE YOU
GO AS LONG
AS YOU
DON'T STOP

IF YOU WANT TO ACHIEVE GRAPENESS, STOP ASKING FOR PERSIMMON

FAZMIEWAR

I THINK YOU ARE SUBLIME

Lettuce always meet each other with smile, for the smile is the beginning of love

MOTHER TERESA

YOU ARE A
PEASHOOTING STAR

YOU
OKALE
HUN?

GOOD THINGS CUMIN GOOD THYME

Peas be gentle on yourself

"SOOOOOME
PEAR OVER THE
RAINBOW"

YIP HARBURG

YOU ARE THE
LIGHT THAT
NEVER GOES
SPROUT

EXIST ON YOUR OWN TURM(ERIC)S*.
THAT IS ALL

For those of you who haven't herb enough, and haven't herb-it-all-bivore, this series has all the chiaing things you've ever wanted to say in vegan-friendly puns* covered.

Find the pearfect gift for any occasion:

I AM GRAPEFUL
all the good thymes I want to
thank you for

YOU ARE MY RAISIN FOR LIVING
words for someone who's
just the pea's knees

DON'T GIVE A FIG
words of wisdom for when
life gives you lemons

YOU ARE 24 CARROT GOLD
words of love for someone who's
worth their weight in root vegetables

WHATAMELON
comforting pick-you-ups
for epic fails

*Or plant-based puns if, like us, you are no longer
sure if avocados are vegan. Or friendly.

I AM
GRAPEFUL

all the good thymes I want to
thank you for

YOU ARE
MY RAISIN
FOR LIVING

words for someone who's
just the pea's knees

DON'T
GIVE A FIG

words of wisdom for when
life gives you lemons

YOU ARE
24 CARROT
GOLD

words of love for someone
who's worth their weight in
root vegetables

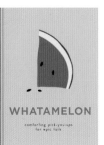

WHATAMELON

comforting pick-you-ups
for epic fails

Acknowledgements and Apologies

With thanks to Andrew, Anna, Steph, Alison and
Matt for their contributions, and special thanks to
Joe as his contributions were really quite good.

We regret not being able to do anything with
cavolo nero, kohl rabi, sorrel and fenugreek.
We hold anyone who can in the highest regard.

"patience is bitter but its fruit is sweet"
ARISTOTLE